Cause his eyes were hazel

Written and illustrated by

Author *M. S. Woodley*

To the family of Patrick Dorismond and the countless men and women of color whose lives were taken by those who swore to protect and serve.

The world was cheated in the greatest way...

On a school night, one of my teammates from High School called on my home phone to tell me that her younger brother was shot and killed exiting a candy store on Flatbush. The first thought that popped in my mind wasn't that he was killed but rather that he was the last person you would expect to be killed. He was an artist; he carried his pencils in his vest pocket-just a very nerdy kid.

It was common knowledge in my neighborhood that when cops killed someone, they'd say that the perpetrator was *"reaching for a gun"*. This was code for *shooting him for no reason*.

I yelled, "So now they are killing nerds!" She responded, "I guess so." Death at the hands of cops was normal in my neighborhood. Came with the territory. In my community, black boys had no value.

Blog post

Author M.S.Woodley

ALL FOUR OF US DESCENDED OFF OF THE BUS,

ONE AFTER THE OTHER.

WE GATHERED TOGETHER BEFORE CROSSING OCEAN AVE.

TO OUR LEFT,

ON THE OPPOSITE SIDE OF THE STREET—

PROSPECT PARK.

ALL OF ITS GREEN WAITED FOR US TO RETURN FROM SCHOOL.

Like little ducklings,
  Oldest to youngest—
    We marched down Parkside Avenue.
    An undiscussed Hierarchy
      An Undisputed chain of
command...

Marie is Patrick's older sister.

They both attended Catholic school.

Isis is my older sister

We went to public school 130.

So Happy –

I did not have to wear a uniform to school

Being able to draw on my clothes

gave me tremendous joy and artistic expression.

THE two OLDER SISTERS
LED the FROnt

OF the LInE.

I LED
tHE MIDDLE.
I
LEANED tOWARDS tHE FRONT,
MIDDLE —FRONT
BUt
not tHE FRONT.
WHERE MARIE AND ISIS WALKED
I NEVER WENt
AND
NEVER tOO FAR tOWARDS tHE BACK.
CLOSER tO tHE FRONt tHEN
tOWARDS tHE BACK
       I tOOK PRIDE IN MY POSITION

THEN THERE WAS PATRICK

                      WAY IN THE BACK...

            WALKING

WITH HIS HEAD POINTED TOWARDS THE GROUND.

    WALKING

AS HE GRAZED THE WALLS WITH HIS HAND,

      WALKING—

            PASSED BY

            THE CANDY STORES AND OTHER BUSINESSES ON THE

RIGHT HAND SIDE OF THE STREET.

And when Marie
gestured for him to catch up...

He would —

But then
 he would fall back.
            Way, way, way in the back
Of us.

IF I HAD A LITTLE BROTHER I WOULD WANT HIM TO BE

LIKE PATRICK.

HE WASN'T LIKE OTHER LITTLE BROTHERS I KNEW.

THEY WERE **HARD HEADED–**

TOO HARD HEADED.

EVERY ONCE IN A WHILE,

I WOULD WAIT FOR PATRICK TO CATCH UP

"HEY" I WOULD SAY.

HE WOULD RESPOND UNDER HIS BREATH, "HELLO".

THEN I WOULD RUN BACK UP —

INTO MY MIDDLE POSITION.

Walking

I turned and looked behind me,

 The bus we just got off of was still behind Patrick.

Every day

The same walk.

     Every day

   He walked a safe distance behind us ...

His hands
Wrapped around the shoulder straps
        on his oversized book bag.
With his head towards the ground.
The sun—
Right there...

WE MARCHED ON TOWARDS FLATBUSH AVE.

WALKING.

SEEMED LIKE THE LONGEST BLOCK...

When we reached Flatbush Avenue,

The green from prospect Park

Was well behind us.

We split up.

While Marie and Patrick waited for the light on
the sidewalk,

My sister and I made a right onto Flatbush.

        "See you tomorrow"

Down Clarkson Avenue we went.

When I started High school,
 I would see Patrick in the
neighborhood.
Several years have passed by.
He has gotten so tall
So Very tall
—no longer a little guy.
I always wondered how this shy
kid would adapt to this Flatbush
environment.
I wondered whether his tremendous
stature —would help or hinder him.
Either way he will be a target...
 My—
What Flatbush does to quiet
younger brothers. To continue to
exist in this environment, He
would have to adapt — He must
adapt—change —harden in some way
— somehow — I wish he could just
remain who he was... Unique.

Students were all shuffled in the auditorium at my High school.

Mayoral Candidate Rodolph Giuliani came to speak to us.

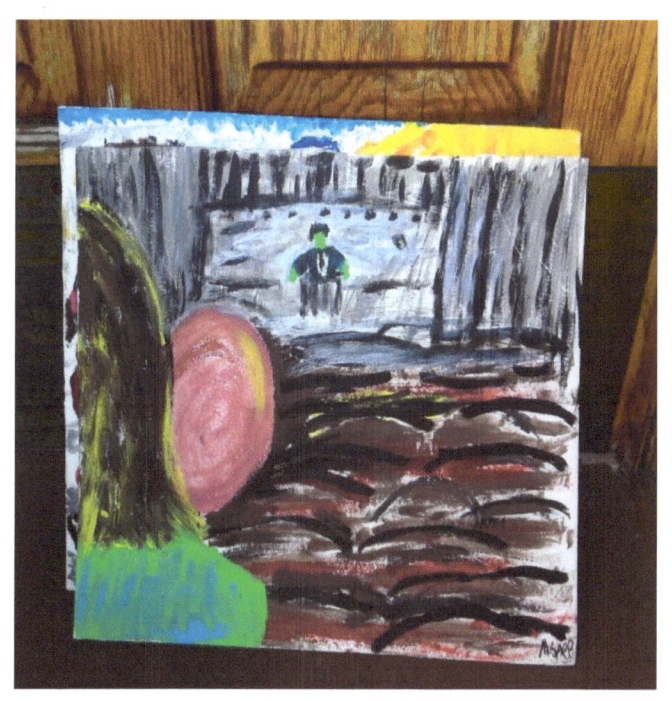

HE AFFIRMED...

     TO KEEP OUR GENERATION SAFE FROM CRIME.
TO PROTECT US STUDENTS.
TO MAKE NYC A SAFER PLACE FOR US THROUGHOUT THE
BOROUGHS.
   HE WENT ON AND ON.
    SUCH WONDERFUL PROMISES,
PROMISES WHICH WILL NEVER REACH
   THE EARS OF THE KIDS IN MY NEIGHBORHOOD.
MUST BE TALKING ABOUT THE KIDS THAT LIVED AROUND MY
HIGH SCHOOL.

I AM HAPPY —

   FOR tHOSE KIDS MATTERED.

MY PROHIBITED GUM CHEWING
 KEPT MY MIND OCCUPIED
AS HE SPOKE.
THE EXCITEMENT OF GETTING CAUGHT
CHEWING MY GUM
 AND BEING TOLD TO SPIT IT OUT,
WAS A DELIBERATE DISTRACTION.
        KEPT MY MIND OFF OF A TRUTH
WHICH—
WEIGHED HEAVY ON MY HEART AND IN MY MIND
 AT FIFTEEN YEARS OLD.

A VERY inconVEniEnt tRutH—
That tHE BLACK KIDS in MY nEIGHBORHOOD— tHEY WERE
JuSt not a PRIORITY. THEY WERE GunnED DOWn WaY too
OFtEn BY COPS. THEY HaD NO VaLuE—NO QUEStions
aSKED.

AS GIuLIani continued HIS SPEECH,
         THE cuRtains BEHIND HIM
 BEGan to CHanGE.
TuRnED into a BLACK anD WHItE FILM.
         HE BEGan to CHanGE COLORS aS WELL.
WItH HIS uncanny RESEMBLanCE to FRanKEnStEin—
     HIS MannERISM — GEStuRES BEHIND tHE PODIUM.
I WatcHED It aLL unFOLD.

AND JUST LIKE THE **1931** MOVIE,
I WATCHED FROM A SAFE DISTANCE.

I OFTEN WONDERED IF GIULIANI VISITED PATRICK'S SCHOOL.

DID HE USE THE SAME SPEECH?

DID HE COMMIT TO KEEPING THE STUDENTS THERE SAFE AS WELL?

I WONDERED IF—

HE KNEW THAT PATRICK READ, ON THE BUS RIDE HOME FROM
SCHOOL.

And On This particular Day,

AS WE WALKED HOME,

THE SKY OPENED UP AND tHE SUN SHINED ON PATRICK WITH SUCH

BOLD PURPOSE.

I WONDERED —

IF HE KNEW —

ON THE CORNER
OF FLATBUSH
AND PARKSIDE
AVE, THAT A TRUTH
REVEALED ITSELF
TO ME...

His eyes—
Yellows,
     Browns,
Greens—
an array of richness,

Which
could only be found in a box of crayons.

DID HE KNOW,

IN HIS EYES

WERE tHOSE crayons—

Lying in a FIELD OF WHEat...

And did he know—
That golden colored peach fuzz
Grew slightly above his brows—
Ascended upon his forehead.
          Met a undefined hair line,
     Which blended into a low cropped fro.

THE GOLDEN
COLORED
PEACH FUZZ ALSO,

RAN DOWN THE NAP OF HIS NECK ...

FOR THIS MOMENT STOOD STILL —
    AS I STARED
AND DISCOVERED,
        A YOUNG PATRICK DORISMOND

HIS SUN KISSED DEEP BROWN SKIN
        WAS tHE COLOR
OF tHE CINNAMON GRAHAM CRACKERS— IN MY POCKEt.

That his top and bottom lip
rested peacefully—
one on top of the other
like
two perfectly fitted puzzle pieces.

On that day
A brother and
son —
stood before
me.
A perfect fruit
born —
of the
universe.

As I sat in the school auditorium,

Watching the picture show—

The movie,

10 years

Passed by so quickly...

I WONDERED,

  IF MAYOR

  GIULIANI KNEW HIS EYES WERE HAZEL.

I WONDERED

IF THEY KNEW.

KNEW THAT HIS EYES —

    WERE THE COLOR OF CRAYONS,

scattered about

in a field of wheat...

and that

under the sun,

his upper and bottom lip

 met together like a child's

warm embrace.

And that he—

Who stood before me —

A brother

And a son.

A perfect fruit—

a gift,

yet to be unwrapped...

Peace and blessings,

M.S. Woodley

Author

About the Author

M.S. Woodley is a workshop leader, professional speaker and blogger. A unique voice in the field of spiritual growth and development, she in an advocate for the use of the Law of Abundance in one's everyday life; having utilized it to overcome her own health crisis. With over fifteen years of implementing programs and services for families of at- risk /high- risk youth in the NYC area, she is a part of a growing movement of Technology- based Entrepreneurs. She resides in Brooklyn, NY.

Contact info: mswoodleyauthor.com
                mswoodleyauthor@gmail.com